This is the story of a real princess who lived over one hundred and fifty years ago.

The Duchess of Kent was
going to have a baby.
"We must go home to
England!" said the Duke.
So they left Germany and travelled
along bumpy roads to England.

When the time came for the baby to be
born, the Duke waited downstairs.
"I am sure it will be a girl," he said.

It was a girl!
The Duke and the Duchess were
very pleased.
"We shall call her Victoria," the Duke said.

When Victoria was only eight months old,
the Duke caught a cold.
Doctors tried to help him by
bleeding him with leeches.

The leeches only made him worse.
As the days passed he grew
weaker and weaker.
Soon he died.

Victoria was a very lonely little girl.
A nurse looked after her all the time.

The nurse took her to see
her mother only at tea time.

She had no friends to play with, so she
played with wooden dolls.
She liked to dress them up.

She had a pet dog called Dash.
She dressed him up too!

When Victoria was five a governess
came to give her lessons.
"I will teach you how to speak French and
German," she said.

One day, the governess told Victoria,
"You must learn to walk with your
head up high."
The governess pinned some holly
under Victoria's chin.
She did not like it at all!

Victoria's Uncle George was the King.
He had a huge belly and eyes like a frog.
Victoria was very fond of him.

One day he asked her, "What is your
favourite tune?"
"God save the King," said Victoria.
King George was so pleased he gave
her a painting of himself set in diamonds.

On her 17th birthday, Cousin Albert
came to visit.
He had come all the way from Germany.
Victoria liked Albert.

When Victoria was 18, the King died.
Victoria became Queen of England.

Victoria married Albert and they had
nine children.
Victoria was Queen for 64 years.